Arctic Ocean

30°E 60° 90° 120° 150°

A S I A

EUROPE

A S

ARABIA

AFRICA

Pacific

Ocean

Indian

Ocean

AUSTRALIA

ANTARCTICA

Countries of the World

Guatemala

Anita Croy

Matthew Taylor and Edwin J. Castellanos, Consultants

NATIONAL GEOGRAPHIC
WASHINGTON, D.C.

Contents

Foreword

I n the following pages you will discover Guatemala, a beautiful country with many contrasts. In a relatively small area, Guatemala offers great geographical and cultural diversity. In a short one-hour trip, you can move from the capital city of Guatemala, which is located high in the mountains at 5,000 feet (1,525 m) and has cool and mild weather, down to the lowlands of the Pacific Coast. There it is hot and humid, and you can sunbathe and swim in the ocean all year round. Or you may travel for the same period of time in another direction from Guatemala City. A one-hour journey up the mountains takes you to the top of an active volcano at 9,000 feet (2,750 m). Here the cold wind mixes with the warm air heated by the lava erupting from the crater.

Just as Guatemala's range of landscapes creates a variety of climates, the country also has a great wealth of culture, with people speaking a number of different languages. A total of 23 ethnic groups make up the population of Guatemala. All of them preserve different traditions and histories, though they are now also linked by the Spanish language, introduced 500 years ago by conquerors from Spain. The time of Spanish rule has left its mark, including many colonial-style buildings. One of the best places to see them is the seemingly timeless city of Antigua.

Guatemalans are proud of their ancestors, the Maya, who were building their empire in the country at the same time Christianity was spreading across Europe. The pyramids and monuments that the Maya built hundreds of years ago stand as a testimony to their great power, knowledge, and skill. They are visited by thousands of tourists every year.

I hope that by reading this book, you will be enchanted by this "Land of Eternal Spring," as the local people call it. You will surely decide to come and experience firsthand the culture, the people, and the beautiful forests and mountains with their abundance of exotic plants and animals. See you soon in Guatemala!

▲ Buses and passengers crowd a bus terminal in Guatemala City, where buses are the only form of public transportation. Many are old school buses imported from the United States.

Edwin Castellanos
Centro de Estudios Ambientales,
Universidad del Valle de Guatemala

Fire
and
Water

NO ONE IS QUITE SURE where Guatemala got its name. Some people suggest it comes from a native word meaning "land of trees," but the country's volcanic landscape suggests another source. The Maya—the country's native people—called one of the volcanoes in their empire *Guhatezmalha*, or "Mountain That Vomits Water." It describes the giant volcano that looms above Antigua Guatemala, one of the country's former capitals.

In 1541 the people of Antigua discovered how the mountain got its ancient name when a torrent of mud rushed down its slopes and swamped the old city. The mudslide was caused by rain-soaked soil created when the volcano erupted. Today, the mountain is known as Volcán de Agua, or "Volcano of Water."

◀ The Volcán de Agua stands to the south of Antigua Guatemala. The mountain is not the only threat to the city. To the west is Volcán de Fuego—"Volcano of Fire."

WHAT'S THE WEATHER LIKE?

The weather in Guatemala varies depending on how high up you are. Much of Guatemala is located at high altitudes, which keeps the temperatures cool. The modern capital, Guatemala City, has an average temperature of 67° F (19° C). The coastal towns are much hotter. The jungles of the Petén in the north are a wet part of the country, receiving 150 inches (380 cm) of rain each year. However, Guatemala also has its own semidesert. Temperatures in the Motagua Valley climb to 100° F (41° C) and rain is rare, making it the driest place in Central America.

The map opposite shows the physical features of Guatemala. Labels on this map and on similar maps throughout this book identify most of the places pictured in each chapter.

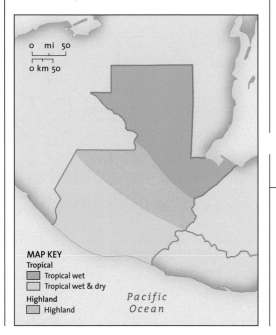

```
o    mi  50
o    km  50
```

MAP KEY
Tropical
- ☐ Tropical wet
- ☐ Tropical wet & dry
Highland
- ☐ Highland

Pacific Ocean

Fast Facts

OFFICIAL NAME: Republic of Guatemala
TYPE OF GOVERNMENT: Democratic Republic
CAPITAL: Guatemala City
POPULATION: 13,002,206
OFFICIAL LANGUAGE: Spanish
MONETARY UNIT: Quetzal
AREA: 42,042 square miles (108,890 square km)
BORDERS: Mexico, Belize, El Salvador, and Honduras
HIGHEST POINT: Volcán Tajumulco, 13,816 feet (4,211 m)
LOWEST POINT: Pacific Ocean, sea level (0 m)
MAJOR MOUNTAIN RANGES: Sierra de las Minas, Sierra de Santa Cruz, Sierra Cuchumatanes
MAJOR RIVERS: Motagua, Usumacinta, Pasión

Average Temperature & Rainfall

Average High/Low Temperatures; Yearly Rainfall
GUATEMALA CITY (CENTER): 90° F (32° C) / 72° F (22° C); 52 inches (132 cm)
FLORES (PETÉN, NORTH): 99° F (37° C) / 59° F (15° C); 150 inches (380 cm)
CHICHICASTENANGO (WEST): 88° F (31° C) / 60° F (16° C); 45 inches (114 cm)

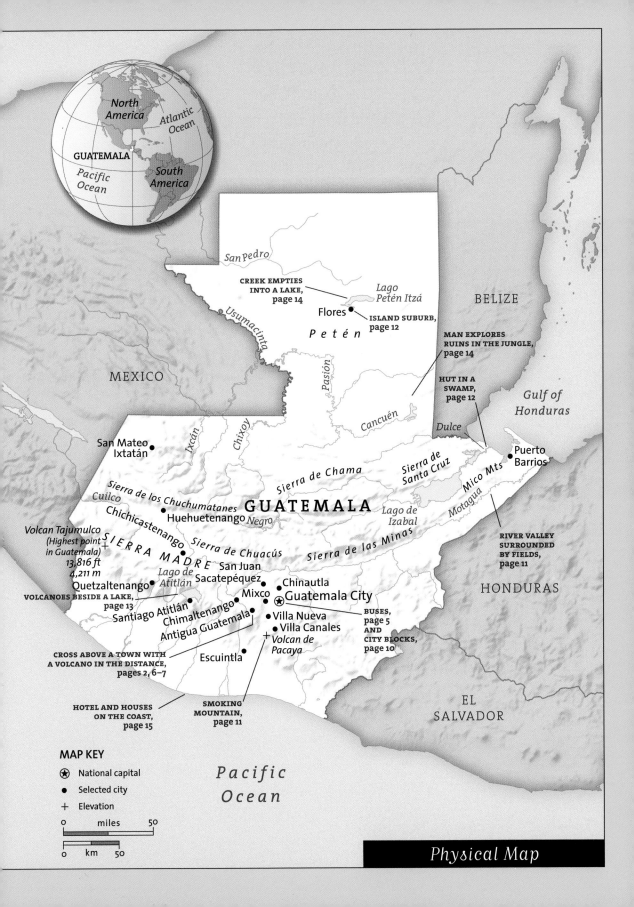

North America

Atlantic
Ocean

GUATEMALA

Pacific
Ocean

South
America

San Pedro

**CREEK EMPTIES
INTO A LAKE,
page 14**

*Lago
Petén Itzá*

BELIZE

Flores

**ISLAND SUBURB,
page 12**

Usumacinta

P e t é n

**MAN EXPLORES
RUINS IN THE JUNGLE,
page 14**

MEXICO

Pasión

Chixoy

Cancuén

**HUT IN A
SWAMP,
page 12**

*Gulf of
Honduras*

Dulce

San Mateo
Ixtatán

Ixcán

Sierra de Chama

*Sierra de
Santa Cruz*

Mico Mts

Puerto
Barrios

Cuilco

Sierra de los Chuchumatanes

GUATEMALA

*Lago de
Izabal*

Motagua

**RIVER VALLEY
SURROUNDED
BY FIELDS,
page 11**

Chichicastenango

Huehuetenango

Negro

*Volcan Tajumulco
(Highest point
in Guatemala)
13,816 ft
4,211 m*

S I E R R A M A D R E

Sierra de Chuacús

Sierra de las Minas

HONDURAS

Quetzaltenango

San Juan
Sacatepéquez

*Lago de
Atitlán*

Chinautla

**VOLCANOES BESIDE A LAKE,
page 13**

Santiago Atitlán

Mixco

Guatemala City

Chimaltenango

**BUSES,
page 5
AND
CITY BLOCKS,
page 10**

Antigua Guatemala

Villa Nueva

Villa Canales

**CROSS ABOVE A TOWN WITH
A VOLCANO IN THE DISTANCE,
pages 2, 6–7**

Escuintla

*Volcan de
Pacaya*

EL
SALVADOR

**HOTEL AND HOUSES
ON THE COAST,
page 15**

**SMOKING
MOUNTAIN,
page 11**

MAP KEY

⊛ National capital

● Selected city

+ Elevation

0   miles   50

0   km   50

*Pacific
Ocean*

Physical Map

Volcanoes and Storms

Guatemala is a small country. It is only a little bigger than the U.S. state of Tennessee. The country is crisscrossed by earthquake faults that often make the ground shake. Over millions of years, many volcanoes have also erupted there. Three of Guatemala's 30 volcanoes are still active, which means they could erupt at any time.

Guatemala has coastlines on both the Pacific Ocean and Caribbean Sea. Hurricanes regularly blow in from the Caribbean and crash onto land. The last major hurricane, Hurricane Mitch, hit Guatemala in 1998 and left 100,000 people homeless. In 2005, Tropical Storm Stan killed more than 600 people.

▲ After two earlier capitals were destroyed by earthquakes and floods, Guatemala City was built in a safer location in the western mountains.

The Shaking Highlands

One-third of Guatemala is mountainous, and most of the population lives in the highlands. The mountains were formed over millions of years as the tectonic plates that lie beneath the country squeezed together. Tectonic plates are the rocky sections that make up Earth's crust. When the plates rub together, they create earthquakes. The main earthquake zone in Guatemala is in the southeast, where the North American Plate rubs against the Caribbean Plate along the Motagua Fault. The region along the fault is shaken by tremors several times each year.

The last major earthquake was in 1976. About 23,000 people were killed. Many villages were wiped out, because homes in the countryside were often made from mud or other weak materials and collapsed very easily. The earthquake happened at about 3:00 A.M. when most people were asleep.

▲ Smoke, steam, and red-hot lava erupt from Pacaya Volcano near Guatemala City. It is the most active volcano in the country.

IN DIFFERENT DIRECTIONS

The mountainous landscape of western Guatemala is built along a backbone of about thirty volcanoes. They extend all the way from the Mexican border in the north to Chingo near the El Salvadoran border in the south. The volcano range includes the most active volcanoes in Central America. Two rivers run through the range—but by a quirk of geography, they both flow in different directions.

The Motagua River flows east toward the Caribbean Sea, while the Chixoy River flows another way. It heads north before emptying into the Usumacinta River and flowing into the Gulf of Mexico. The Motagua River starts in the mountains north of Guatemala City, and follows the Motagua Fault for 250 miles (400 km) until it spills into Omoa Bay.

▲ The banks of the Motagua River are ideal places for farms among the rugged mountains.

Smoke Rising

Guatemala's active volcanoes stand close to the faults between the tectonic plates. They frequently threaten to burst into life. In 1902, the Santa Maria volcano erupted with devastating effects. Thousands were killed as ash from the volcano spread over hundreds of square miles. The Pacaya Volcano, near Guatemala City, never stops smoking. Its last major eruption was in 2007.

▲ **This exclusive suburb of the city of Flores in the north of the country has been built on an island in the middle of Lake Petén Iztá.**

Deep Holes

Over millions of years, Guatemala's volcanic activity has created hollows in the landscape that have been filled by rivers to form large lakes. The country's largest lake (the third largest lake in Central America) is Lake Izabal.

SWEET RIVER TO RICHES

The largest lake in Guatemala, Lake Izabal, lies close to the Gulf of Honduras, which is an inlet of the Caribbean Sea. The Rio Dulce, or Sweet River, links the lake to the gulf through a spectacular gorge. Both the Rio Dulce and Lake Izabal are fairly shallow and easily navigated. During Spanish colonial rule, the lake served as a harbor for galleons, or ships, preparing to take gold, jewels, and other treasures back to Spain. Pirates often raided ships on the lake, and sunk many of the galleons. The wrecks still lie around the mouth of the river.

▲ **The Rio Dulce passes through jungle where few people live.**

It is a basin that was formed between two mountain ranges near the Caribbean Coast.

Guatemala's most famous lake is Lake Atitlán. Its beautiful mountain setting makes it a popular tourist attraction. The other major Guatemalan lake is Lake Petén Itzá, in the lowlands of the north.

Flat Lands

Among the mountains and volcanoes of Guatemala are two large areas of lowland. The Pacific lowland runs along the southern coast. The area is sandwiched between the mountains and ocean. Rivers feed the lowlands making them a very fertile area.

The other lowland area is much bigger. Known as El Petén, the region covers the whole of northeastern Guatemala. The landscape is covered in small limestone hills. Limestone is

CRATER LAKE

When the British writer Aldous Huxley visited Guatemala in the 1950s, he called Lake Atitlán "the most beautiful lake in the world." Atitlán is also the deepest lake in Central America. Its exact depth is still not known precisely, but it is thought to be about 900 feet (300 m). Around 84,000 years ago, a massive volcano exploded on the site with such force that it sent volcanic ash as far away as Florida. When the dust settled, the volcano had collapsed into the ground, creating a wide basin called a caldera. New volcanoes formed beside the caldera, stopping water from flowing out of it and creating Lake Atitlán. Today the lake covers 48 square miles (125 square km)— but it is mysteriously losing water. One theory is that a 1976 earthquake opened up a passage in the lake bed that is allowing water to seep out.

▲ Lake Atitlán is more than a mile above sea level in the Sierra de Chuacús. Its natural beauty has made it a popular tourist destination.

easily eroded by water. The water seeps into cracks in the rocks and slowly dissolves it from the inside. As a result this area is full of caves and sinkholes. Areas of harder rock erode more slowly, so they often form steep-sided hills and towers.

▲ The Petén is full of Mayan ruins that have been hidden in the jungle for centuries.

The Petén covers a third of Guatemala's total area, but only about 3 percent of Guatemalans live there. Much of the land is swampy jungle, which is too difficult to convert into farmland. However, more people are moving to this empty region in search of

HIDDEN WATER

While some parts of the Petén are dry, much of it is swampy. Rivers and creeks do not make it to the sea. Instead, their water disappears into underground caves in the eroded landscape. Some of it ends up in Lake Petén Itzá.

Lake Petén Itzá fills a depression in a limestone plateau. It is fed by creeks from the east, but they alone do not carry enough water to fill the lake. It is also filled with water from far underground: the lake is 165 feet (50 m) deep. The constant supply of freshwater in the lake helped the Maya live in the area and avoid being conquered by the Spaniards until 1697.

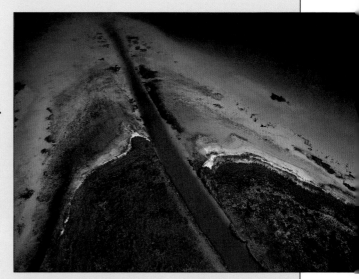

▲ One of many small narrow creeks carries water into Lake Petén Itzá.

land. As a result, deforestation is becoming an increasing problem as farmers and ranchers clear the trees. The land cannot support crops or pastures for more than a few years, so the settlers are forced to move on regularly and clear more of the jungle for land.

Double Coasts

Guatemala has eastern and southern coastlines facing separate oceans. The Caribbean coast is shorter, at only about 60 miles (100 km). It is located around the mouths of the Motagua River and Rio Dulce, where the country is squeezed between Belize and Honduras.

On the other side of the country, the coast runs for about 150 miles (240 km) along the Pacific Ocean. The mountains rise a few miles from the Pacific Coast. They are pushed up where the Pacific's tectonic plate plunges under the land. The land along the coast is used for farming. Large areas of tropical rain forest have been converted into huge farms. The climate at sea level is very warm, which makes it ideal for growing sugarcane and fruit.

▲ Luxury hotels and traditional towns stand side-by-side on Guatemala's rugged southern coast.

Hidden Colors

HIGH UP IN CLOUD FORESTS that cover Guatemala's mountains lives the resplendent quetzal. One of the most beautiful birds in the world, the quetzal is very distinctive. Both the male and female have green, red, and white bodies—but the male also has a spectacular tail that can be up to 3 feet (1 m) long. Despite their plumage, the birds are well camouflaged while they feed on their favorite food, avocados. Their feathers only turn bright in direct sunlight; otherwise, their bodies are quite dull and hide easily among the leaves.

The quetzal is sacred to the Maya. The Guatemalan currency is even named after the bird. However, the destruction of Guatemala's tropical forests means that these amazing birds are now officially endangered.

◀ Ancient people believed that the resplendent quetzal was the living form of the god Quetzalcoatl. The bird's tail feathers were used in religious ceremonies.

WILD LAND

Guatemala's swamps, mountains, and coastlines give it a wide variety of habitats. The map opposite shows the vegetation zones—or what grows where—in Guatemala.

There are more than 250 kinds of mammals in the country, ranging from the elusive mountain lion and jaguar to the strange-looking tapir. Monkeys are seen all over the country, including howlers and spider monkeys. At least 750 species of birds live in Guatemala. In addition to the quetzal, there are parrots, macaws, eagles, and hummingbirds. Some species are now extinct, however, including the giant grebe of Lake Atitlán. When largemouth bass were introduced to the lake in 1958, they ate all the smaller fish, leaving nothing for the giant grebe to eat. By 1986, it was extinct.

Guatemala's varied ecosystems contain thousands of plant species. Forests grow in the swampy Petén region, while cacti cover the desert regions. The country's wildflowers include arum lilies and 550 types of orchid. The national flower is the *monja blanca* orchid—"the white nun."

▶ A male Jaribú stork carries twigs back to his nest. This species is one of the largest birds living in Guatemala—when fully grown it stands 5 feet (1.5 m) tall.

Species at Risk

While rain forests elsewhere in the Americas have largely been cleared, Guatemala's forests and the wildlife within them have continued to thrive because much of the country is only lightly populated. There are also nearly 100 protected areas that range from national parks visited by large numbers of tourists to remote wilderness areas that receive few visitors. However, today some areas are under threat from mining and logging. Both the Pacific coast and the Petén have lost much of their natural habitat. Species at risk include:

> American manatee
> Baird's tapir
> Big long-nosed bat
> Central American woolly opossum
> Giant anteater
> Guatemalan myotis (bat)
> Maya mouse
> Southern long-nosed bat

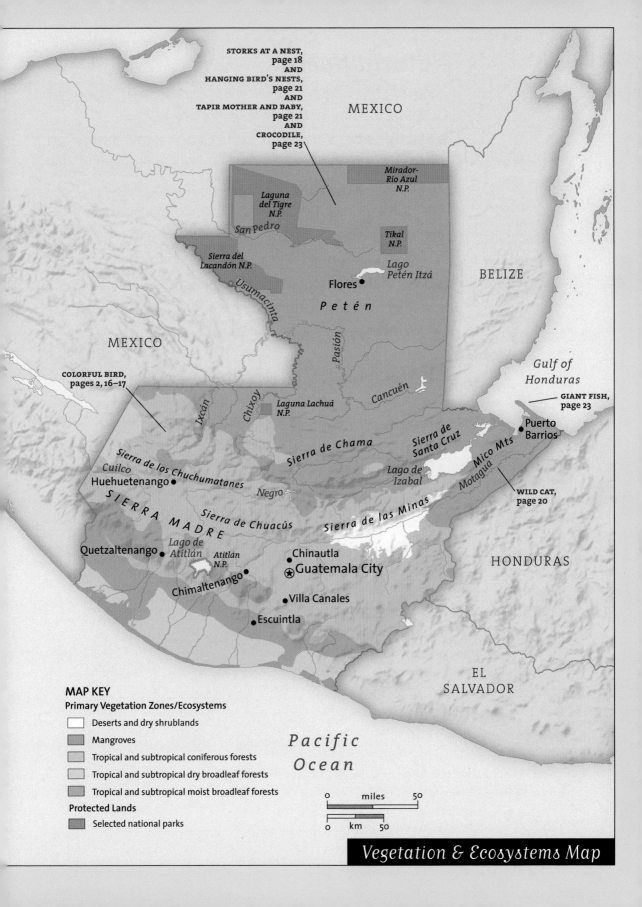

STORKS AT A NEST,
page 18
AND
HANGING BIRD'S NESTS,
page 21
AND
TAPIR MOTHER AND BABY,
page 21
AND
CROCODILE,
page 23

MEXICO

Mirador-
Río Azul
N.P.

Laguna
del Tigre
N.P.

San Pedro

Sierra del
Lacandón N.P.

Tikal
N.P.

BELIZE

Usumacinta

Flores

Lago
Petén Itzá

P e t é n

MEXICO

COLORFUL BIRD,
pages 2, 16–17

Pasión

Gulf of
Honduras

GIANT FISH,
page 23

Ixcán

Chixoy

Laguna Lachuá
N.P.

Cancuén

Sierra de Chama

Sierra de
Santa Cruz

Mico Mts

Puerto
Barrios

Sierra de los Chuchumatanes

Cuilco

Huehuetenango

Negro

Lago de
Izabal

Motagua

WILD CAT,
page 20

S I E R R A   M A D R E

Sierra de Chuacús

Sierra de las Minas

HONDURAS

Quetzaltenango

Lago de
Atitlán

Atitlán
N.P.

Chinautla

Guatemala City

Chimaltenango

Villa Canales

Escuintla

EL
SALVADOR

Pacific
Ocean

MAP KEY
Primary Vegetation Zones/Ecosystems

- Deserts and dry shrublands
- Mangroves
- Tropical and subtropical coniferous forests
- Tropical and subtropical dry broadleaf forests
- Tropical and subtropical moist broadleaf forests

Protected Lands

- Selected national parks

0   miles   50

0   km   50

Vegetation & Ecosystems Map

Natural Home

There are more than 19 different ecosystems in Guatemala. They include mangrove forests and wetlands on both coasts, as well as tropical rain forests and swamps in the Petén region. There are oak and pine forests and grassy meadows on the lower hills. The higher slopes are covered in cloud forests, or wet, tropical forests that are often shrouded in the mist that covers high mountains. More than one-quarter of the country is protected through a system of wildlife refuges, national parks, and privately owned nature reserves.

Misty Mountaintops

Cloud forests grow in Guatemala up to about 11,700 feet (3,500 m). Above that altitude the

THE GRAY ONE

Lurking on the banks of Guatemala's forest rivers is a strange species of cat. The jaguarundi often does not look much like a cat. Its short legs and small head make it look more like a weasel or otter. It is often called the "otter cat." The jaguarundi is an expert fisher, using its front paws to snatch fish from the water. Like other small cats across the world, it also eats birds and mice. The jaguarundi hunts alone and spends the rest of its time snoozing in the branches of trees.

The color of the cat's hair depends on its habitat. Jaguarundis living in dense forest have dark red fur. In drier habitats, they are gray. *Jaguarundi* means "the gray one." When first born, the cats have spots, but these fade at around four months.

▲ The jaguarundi grows to about 30 inches (65 cm) long.

habitat changes to barren rock.

The mountain mist provides a constant source of water for the plants that grow there. Bromeliads cling to tree trunks. Known as air plants, they absorb water directly from the misty air instead of being rooted in the ground. Vines snake around the many trees, and the forest floor is covered with orchids, ferns, and mosses.

About 145 bird species have been counted in the different cloud forest regions, including the quetzal, the national symbol. The forest floor is ruled by the puma, or mountain lion, which hunts for squirrels, rats, and other small game like brocket deer.

In the Petén

The vast lowland of the Petén is one of the richest places in Guatemala for animal and plant life. Along the jungle floor, the vibrantly colored oscillated turkey struts around like a peacock. High up in the trees, birds such as Montezuma's Oropendola and toucan fly around the forest canopy. Many different kinds of water birds, including the

DRAGON FRUIT

Imagine eating a fruit that has bright pink skin with scales sticking out of it! But cut the fruit open, and you will see tasty white flesh dotted with black seeds. This is a dragon fruit. It grows on a large cactus called a pitaya, which is native to Central America.

The flowers of the pitaya are large and white. They only open at night, which earns the cactus the alternative name of moonflower. The flowers have a strong scent that attracts bats and moths to pollinate the plants.

▶ Dragon fruit is likened in flavor to a mild kiwifruit.

pied-billed grebe, herons, and jacana wade in the waters of the Petén's many lakes.

The region's large plant-eating animals include tapirs and mule deer, which browse the forest floor. The peccary also digs through the fallen leaves for food. The peccary looks like a wild boar, but is only a distant relation of hogs.

The leaves and fruits higher up the trees are eaten by howler monkeys, which are named for the hooting calls they make to ward off rivals. Monkeys and other animals fall prey to the Petén's hunters, which include the mighty jaguar and the ocelot, a smaller wild cat.

Off Shore

Guatemala's Caribbean coast is home to more than 350 species of birds, plus many that visit on yearly migrations. They include the woodthrush and blue-winged warbler. Other visitors to the Caribbean coast include the manatee—an unusual sea mammal whose closest relative is the elephant—and the American crocodile, a giant reptile that can survive in both freshwater and the ocean. Both of these species are becoming increasingly rare. Birds such as great egrets, roseate spoonbills, and belted kingfishers live along the

SMOOTH KILLER

In Guatemala's lakes and rivers lurks an efficient killer—the Morelet crocodile. Compared with other crocodiles, the Morelet is small, but adults can still grow to 10 feet (3 m) long! The Morelet has a wider snout than other crocodiles, which makes it look more like an alligator. Morelet crocodiles also have very smooth skin on their bellies that people use for making boots and purses. Human trappers have nearly driven the crocodile to extinction. To meet the demand for its skin today, and to protect those that still live in the wild, the Morelet crocodile is raised in farms.

▲ Guatemala's crocodiles live mainly in the Petén swamps.

Pacific coast. Some Pacific beaches are protected as nesting sites for turtles. Species such as the leatherback, olive ridley, and Baule sea turtles all bury their eggs in the sand on the beaches and leave them to hatch.

▼ The world's largest fish, the whale shark, lives off Guatemala's Caribbean coast. Although it can be 60 feet (20 m) long, this giant is harmless to people.

Lost
and
Found

THE STEPS of the Temple of the Jaguar lead 144 feet (44 m) above the Great Plaza in the Mayan city of Tikal, deep in the rain forest of the Petén. The temple was built over 1,300 years ago as a tomb for the ruler of Tikal, Ah Cacaw. Beyond the Great Plaza stood more than 3,000 temples, palaces, and houses. The city went into decline around 850 A.D. for reasons that are still a mystery. About fifty years later, the Maya abandoned Tikal altogether. The jungle swallowed up the buildings. It was not until 1695 that a lost traveler stumbled across the Great Plaza. The Spaniards who then governed the region were not interested in ruins. It was 150 years later that the temples were found to be part of an entire city. Today, Tikal is Guatemala's most important tourist destination.

◀ **The Temple of the Jaguar rises above the Great Plaza at Tikal. The ruined city that rises from the jungle today dates from the 10th century A.D.**

ANCIENT CIVILIZATIONS

Archaeologists believe that people have been living in Guatemala since early humans crossed the Bering Strait from Asia and spread through the Americas about 14,000 years ago. The earliest physical evidence of human settlements in Guatemala dates back to around 9000 B.C. Archaeologists have unearthed stone tools and spear tips at sites in the highlands. The finds show that early Guatemalans lived as hunting and fishing nomads. Around 1000 B.C., people started to settle in villages and grow crops, such as corn, squash, and beans. Some of these early Guatemalans became the Maya, who came to dominate the country's early history. The height of their power came between A.D. 250 and 900. At its peak, the Mayan Empire stretched from Guatemala across Central America and southern Mexico.

▶ This Mayan clay statuette is hollow—it was used as a whistle.

Time line

This chart shows some of the important dates in Guatemalan history.

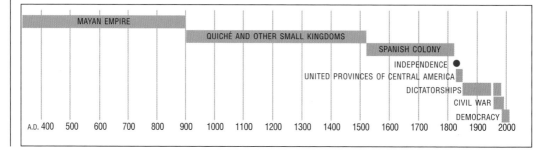

MAYAN EMPIRE

QUICHÉ AND OTHER SMALL KINGDOMS

SPANISH COLONY

INDEPENDENCE ●

UNITED PROVINCES OF CENTRAL AMERICA

DICTATORSHIPS

CIVIL WAR

DEMOCRACY

A.D. 400   500   600   700   800   900   1000   1100   1200   1300   1400   1500   1600   1700   1800   1900   2000

Gulf of Mexico

M E X I C O

CLAY STATUETTE,
page 26
AND
ANCIENT PAINTING,
page 28

El Mirador ◆   Río Azul ◆

MAYAN CITY,
page 29

Uaxactún ◆

STEPPED PYRAMIDS,
pages 2-3, 24-25

Tikal ◆

● Flores

B E L I Z E

Usumacinta

MAYAN PEOPLE
OUTSIDE CHURCH,
page 33

Altar de Sacrificios ◆

Chixoy

Gulf of Honduras

CHILDREN IN COSTUMES,
page 30
AND
MAN IN TRADITIONAL CLOTHING,
page 30

G U A T E M A L A

Lago de Izabal

Motagua

Quiriguá ◆

WORKERS IN
BANANA PLANTATION,
page 34

Negro

H O N D U R A S

Quetzaltenango ●

Mixco ●

Chimaltenango ●

● Guatemala City

Antigua Guatemala ●

● Escuintla

HISTORIC CITY PLAZA,
page 34
AND
SOLDIER GIVING A SPEECH,
page 35

RUINED CATHEDRAL,
page 31

EL SALVADOR

Pacific Ocean

Historical Map

Amazing Maya

The Maya were the most advanced civilization in Guatemala. They made many remarkable achievements in math and astronomy. Their buildings show that they used advanced construction techniques, even though they had no metal tools. The Maya built huge cities using only tools made of stone. They were also skilled farmers. They used complex irrigation systems to water their fields so that they could grow enough food for the population. The lowland city of Tikal was one of the Maya's most impressive cities. At its peak, it was home to 100,000 people and covered 222 square miles (576 sq. km).

▲ A Mayan hieroglyph, or writing symbol, appears on a pot found near the Rio Azul.

▼ A Mayan incense burner in the shape of a warrior god that is half man, half bird

Mayan Life and Death

Much of what we know about the Maya comes from their craftwork, such as sculptures, pottery, and weaving. But the Maya also left written records. They wrote using hieroglyphs, or symbols that represent both sounds and whole words. Experts have learned how to understand the hieroglyphs to learn about Mayan history and way of life.

For example, they have discovered that the Maya were often at war with their neighbors. Prisoners of war were rarely allowed to go home after the end of the fighting—the Maya sacrificed them to their gods.

European Conquerors

The Mayan Empire began to shrink in the 10th century. For the next 600 years, the history of Guatemala is something of a mystery. The Maya split into smaller groups. The Quiché emerged as the strongest power. But even the Quiché were no match for a new power that arrived in the region in the 16th century: Spanish soldiers who came seeking gold and other treasure. Hernan Cortés, who had conquered Mexico, sent Pedro de Alvarado south to Guatemala. Alvarado arrived in 1523 with 400 men. A force of 30,000

WHERE DID THEY GO?

Historians have long puzzled over what caused the decline of the Maya Empire. It began shrinking long before the Spanish arrived, and no other power took control of the region. One popular theory is that a severe drought led to mass starvation. Another theory is that there were just too many Maya for the amount of food farmers could grow. The different Maya groups often fought each other and their neighbors, so perhaps a series of disastrous defeats led to a loss of territory and depletion of resources.

▲ An artist's impression of how Mirador, a Mayan city in the Petén, looked in about 100 B.C.

Quiché attacked—but they were no match for the Spaniards. The newcomers used guns and fought on horseback, both of which were unknown in the Americas at the time.

Children dress up as conquistadors, or Spanish conquerors, during a town fair.

A Spanish Colony

Guatemala became part of the Spanish colony of New Spain. It turned out to have little gold or treasure. Instead, Spanish colonists turned the lowlands into vast estates known as *encomiendas*. They forced the Quiché to work on the farms as slaves. The encomienda owners became so rich that in 1542 Carlos V of Spain banned all forced labor in his empire to make sure that the landowners did not become too influential.

The colony thrived. The Spaniards built settlements based on towns in Spain. Even today, Guatemalan towns have the same shape. The towns are built around a central plaza, or square; the houses are built around courtyards.

The Spaniards also influenced religion. Roman Catholic priests arrived to convert local people to

▼ A Quiché leader wears traditional dress and carries a ceremonial staff.

Christianity. The Catholic Church in Guatemala had its own plantations and soon became rich and powerful. Many Mayan people adopted the new religion, but they did not give up their traditional beliefs. They worshipped both their own gods and Christian saints.

Independence!

Guatemala was a Spanish colony for almost 300 years. But by the start of the 19th century, many parts of Spain's American empire wanted to be independent. Their citizens did not want to be governed by Spain. In many places, independence came after violent rebellion and warfare. However, Guatemala declared independence peacefully in 1821.

Immediately the new country faced a serious threat from its neighbor Mexico, which briefly took it over.

RED EXPORT

When the Spaniards first arrived in Guatemala, they were amazed at the red color of local peoples' clothes. The red was deeper and richer than any dye they had back in Europe. They thought it must come from some kind of plant. In fact, the dye—cochineal—came from bugs. Local Indians had used it for hundreds of years.

The dye was so valuable that the Spaniards built large plantations of cactus plants for the bugs to live on. They used local people to raise the bugs and harvest the pigment. It was a tricky process. The insects had to be kept warm and the plants had to be protected from disease. Cooking and drying the insects caused chemical changes to produce a deep maroon pigment. For 250

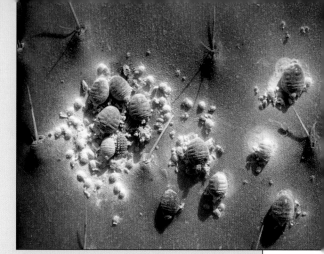

▲ Cochineal bugs look like mold on leaves, but they are insects that suck the juice from the cactus.

years, the Spaniards dominated the trade in cochineal, which was so highly prized in Europe that it helped make Spain one of the richest nations on Earth. Today, cochineal is mainly used to dye foods.

But then Guatemala became part of a separate country in 1823 called the United Provinces of Central America. This union covered all of Central America, but it broke up into the region's present-day countries in 1840.

Political Struggles

Since Guatemala gained its independence, it has been split between two groups: the Conservatives, who represented the interests of the church and wealthy landowners, and the Liberals, who wanted a more equal society. The first president of Guatemala was elected in 1844. He was José Rafael Carrera, a Conservative. Carrera's links to the landowners and bishops kept him in power until his death in 1865.

In 1873, Justo Rufino Barrios, a Liberal, came to power as an unelected dictator. Barrios was the first of many military dictators to seize control of Guatemala.

Business Boom

Guatemala's economy boomed in the 1870s, mainly thanks to coffee. By 1885, coffee made up more than 80 percent of the country's exports. Ancient Maya communities were forced off their land to make way for coffee plantations.

Life for most Guatemalans was still tough. Most of the wealth was in the hands of a few landowners. At

▲ Villagers crowd outside a church in the western mountains of Guatemala to watch an Easter parade with a mix of Mayan and Catholic traditions.

ANOTHER UNITED STATES?

After independence, Guatemala was briefly part of the Mexican Empire. When it broke away from its northern neighbor in 1823, Guatemala became a state in the United Provinces of Central America. The other states included Costa Rica, Honduras, Nicaragua, and El Salvador. Guatemala City was made the new country's capital.

The United Provinces was modeled after the system of government used in the United States of America. The members of the federation hoped that by working together their small countries would grow into one powerful nation. However, from the start the union was split by power struggles. Political differences among the states eventually broke the union apart in 1840.

▲ Manuel Jose Arce was the first president of the United Provinces of Central America.

BANANA REPUBLIC

Today, bananas are a favorite food, but in the 19th century they were a valuable luxury. In 1871, an American businessman named Minor Keith began growing bananas in Central America. His company, the United Fruit Company (UFC), was hugely successful. By the 1930s, the UFC controlled all of Guatemala's railroads and coffee industry. It also had great influence over the country's leaders—but it did not pay any taxes to the national government. Guatemalans called the company El Pulpo, meaning "The Octopus," because its power spread across the country like tentacles.

▲ Workers wait to load bananas onto a train at a UFC plantation in 1926.

Today, the term "banana republic" is still used to describe a weak government whose economy depends on one or two businesses that are controlled by a foreign country.

▼ The National Palace of Culture (left) stands opposite the much older cathedral (right) at Guatemala City's Parque Central. The palace was built by Jorge Ubico in the 1940s using forced labor.

the end of the 19th century another dictator, Manuel Estrada Cabrera, let foreign companies take control of Guatemala's largest industries.

In 1931, President Jorge Ubico assumed power. He passed a new law that forced people with no land to work for 150 days a year for the local landowner or to build roads or do other work for the government. Ubico was overthrown in 1944 and replaced by a democratically elected leader, Juan José Arévalo.

Coups and Conflicts

In 1951, Jacobo Arbenz Guzman was elected president in Arévalo's place. He began to redistribute land, taking it from large businesses and giving it to farmers. The changes angered the landowners, including the huge American-owned United Fruit Company. The U.S. government feared that Arbenz would make Guatemala a communist country. It supported a plot that removed him from power in 1954. Arbenz's reforms were reversed. However, a group named the Armed Rebel Forces began to fight for a return to democratic government. The United States supported the Guatemalan army against the rebels. The fighting lasted until 1996; more than 200,000 people died.

Peace at Last

Peace talks between the government and the rebels started in 1987, but it was not until nine years later that the treaty was finally signed and peace came to Guatemala. Since then, the new Guatemalan government has tried to make sure that war criminals from both sides face justice. It has also again adopted policies aimed at trying to give Mayan communities more control over their land.

▲ The military junta, or committee, that seized power in Guatemala in 1982 announced the change in government. General Efrain Rios Monti, leader of the junta, appears at the center. He was overthrown 16 months later by other military commanders.

Living *with* History

GUATEMALA HAS A HISTORY that is still very much alive today. The country's native people include the direct descendants of the Maya who lived in the mighty empire 1,000 years ago. In some parts of rural Guatemala, everyday life has changed little since those days. The Maya wear the same brightly colored woven clothes their ancestors once wore; they eat the same food and pray to the same gods. They celebrate their many holy days with special festivals.

Life in Guatemala City is very different. The modern capital is the largest city in Central America. Its downtown districts have luxury high-rise apartment buildings and expensive cars on the streets. But even after years of war in the late 20th century, most of Guatemala's wealth is still in the hands of a lucky few.

◄ **A Guatemalan girl poses with her bike in the city of Tecún Umán.**

LIVING HERITAGE

Guatemala has the largest percentage of indigenous people of any Central American country. More than half of the 13.5 million population are Maya. There are about 20 Mayan groups. The million-strong Quiché are the largest. Most of them live in and around the city of Quetzaltenango. The smallest Mayan group is the Xinca. Only 250 of them live near the border with El Salvador. The Garífuna people are descended from Maya and African slaves. They live on the Caribbean coast. Ladinos have mixed Mayan and European heritage.

▲ Quiché dancers dress in bull costumes during a performance in Quetzaltenango.

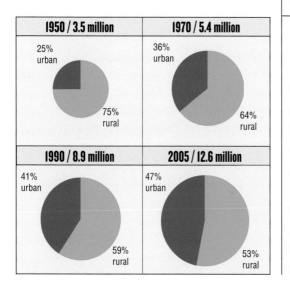

1950 / 3.5 million	1970 / 5.4 million
25% urban / 75% rural	36% urban / 64% rural
1990 / 8.9 million	2005 / 12.6 million
41% urban / 59% rural	47% urban / 53% rural

Common Spanish Phrases

There are about 20 languages spoken in Guatemala, mostly different types of Mayan dialect. Spanish is the official language but the most important government documents are also written in the Mayan languages, including the 1996 peace treaty. Most Guatemalans can speak Spanish. Here are some Spanish phrases for you to try:

Good morning	Buenos días
How are you?	¿Cómo está usted?
Good to meet you	Mucho gusto
See you later	Hasta luego

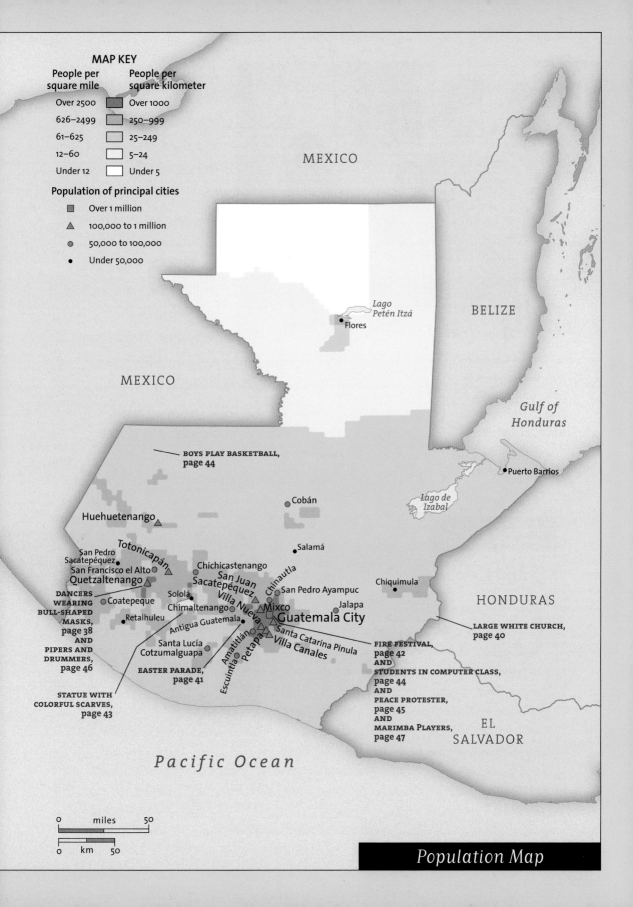

MAP KEY

People per square mile		People per square kilometer
Over 2500		Over 1000
626–2499		250–999
61–625		25–249
12–60		5–24
Under 12		Under 5

Population of principal cities

■ Over 1 million

▲ 100,000 to 1 million

● 50,000 to 100,000

• Under 50,000

MEXICO

BELIZE

Lago Petén Itzá

• Flores

MEXICO

Gulf of Honduras

BOYS PLAY BASKETBALL, page 44

• Puerto Barrios

● Cobán

Huehuetenango ▲

Lago de Izabal

● Salamá

Totonicapán ▲

San Pedro Sacatepéquez •

Chichicastenango ●

San Juan Sacatepéquez ▲

Chinautla

San Francisco el Alto ●

San Pedro Ayampuc •

Chiquimula •

Quetzaltenango ▲

Sololá ●

Villa Nueva ▲

Mixco

HONDURAS

DANCERS WEARING BULL-SHAPED MASKS, page 38 AND PIPERS AND DRUMMERS, page 46

● Coatepeque

Chimaltenango ●

Guatemala City

Jalapa ●

LARGE WHITE CHURCH, page 40

• Retalhuleu

Antigua Guatemala ●

Santa Catarina Pinula

Amatitlán ●

Santa Lucía Cotzumalguapa ●

Escuintla ●

Petapa

Villa Canales

FIRE FESTIVAL, page 42 AND STUDENTS IN COMPUTER CLASS, page 44 AND PEACE PROTESTER, page 45 AND MARIMBA PLAYERS, page 47

EASTER PARADE, page 41

STATUE WITH COLORFUL SCARVES, page 43

EL SALVADOR

Pacific Ocean

0	miles	50

0	km	50

Population Map

Life Together

Most Guatemalans think family is one of the most important things in life. Family life and the extended village community are at the heart of the traditional Mayan way of life. Families usually work and live together. They often

▲ The female members of three generations of a Guatemalan family pose outside their home: a grandmother, her daughters, and their children.

gather together for weekend meals and fiestas— village parties held to celebrate religious festivals.

Guatemalan families are often large; most parents have three or four children. As Guatemalans get better healthcare, people live longer and fewer children die from disease. As a result, the population

BLACK CHRIST OF ESQUIPULAS

Close to the border with El Salvador is the small town of Esquipulas. It is one of the most important pilgrimage sites in Latin America. Inside the large white church, built by the Spanish, hangs a statue of Jesus Christ on the cross. It is carved from dark wood, which is why it is known as the Black Christ. Its fame began in 1737. A story said that the Archbishop of Guatemala visited the church and was cured of a horrible sickness when he touched the statue. Word spread of the miracle, and pilgrims have flocked to the church ever since to pray to the statue and ask for help.

▲ The church at Esquipulas is large enough to hold hundreds of pilgrims.

is one of the fastest growing in the world. About 40 percent of Guatemalans are under 15.

Religious Differences

Since the Spaniards arrived in Central America in the 16th century, Roman Catholicism has been the main religion across the region. About 90 percent of Latin Americans are Catholic. However, the proportion of Catholics in Guatemala is much lower—only about 50 percent are Catholic.

Many Guatemalans are Protestant. A form of Christianity called Evangelical Protestantism is the fastest-growing religion in the country. There are also tiny Jewish and Muslim communities in Guatemala City started by immigrants who came from Eastern Europe, Syria, and Lebanon in the 20th century.

Another religion is unique to the Maya Indians. Over the centuries, the Maya of the Guatemalan highlands have combined traditional beliefs

NATIONAL HOLIDAYS

Most of the public holidays in Guatemala are part of the Roman Catholic calendar. Each town celebrates its own saint's day. The great events in the nation's history, such as the declaration of independence, are also holidays.

▲ A red-robed statue of Christ is carried in a procession during the Easter Holy Week. The procession follows a route decorated by patterns made with colored sawdust.

JANUARY 1	New Year's Day
JANUARY 6	Epiphany
MARCH/APRIL	Easter
MAY 1	Labor Day
JUNE 30	Army Day
AUGUST 15	Assumption
SEPTEMBER 15	Independence Day
OCTOBER 20	Revolution Day
NOVEMBER 1	All Saints' Day
DECEMBER 24	Christmas Eve
DECEMBER 25	Christmas Day
DECEMBER 31	New Year's Eve

with Catholicism. This kind of combination of a religion with traditional beliefs is known as syncretism.

Natural Beliefs

The Maya believe that natural features such as rivers, mountains, and caves are sacred. In some rural churches, people make offerings to Catholic saints using candles and then sacrifice chickens on the church floors for the Mayan gods. Just before Christmas, on December 7, is a festival called Quema del Diablo or "Burning the Devil." The festival is another mixture of Catholic and Mayan beliefs. People make huge fires and burn figures of the devil.

Archaeologists know about the roots of Mayan traditions thanks to several Mayan texts that still survive. The most important is called the Popol Vuh. Quiché leaders wrote this sacred book around the middle of the 16th century to record their beliefs,

▼ Statues representing the devil are burned at a fire festival held in Guatemala on December 7 each year.

WHEN A GOD COMES TO VISIT

Playing cards at a table, dressed in black, with a fedora hat on his head and colorful scarves around his neck, is one of the most unlikely gods in the world. This is Maximón, a statue that is kept in Santiago Atitlán, a village in the western highlands.

Local people worship Maximón to ensure good harvests. Maximón lives in a villager's house. Every Easter, he is given a bath and fresh clothes before moving to a new home in the village. Maximón's new room is decorated with plastic dolls and flashing lights. The god is seated at a table with a glass of rum, a fresh cigar, and a deck of cards to see him through the year.

▲ Maximón moves to a new house on Easter.

which had been passed down by word of mouth for centuries. The Popol Vuh was written on bark paper. When the Spanish conquerors arrived, they burned many of the Mayan texts—but the Popol Vuh survived.

▼ Carlos Ruíz, Guatemala's top soccer star, in action in the United States

The Little Fish

Like most other Latin Americans, Guatemalans love soccer (known as *fútbol*). It is their favorite sport to watch, and on Sundays many men and boys play in amateur leagues. The most famous Guatemalan soccer player is Carlos Ruíz. He is widely known as El Pescadito ("The Little Fish") because of the way he can wriggle through

the other side's defense. Ruíz has played in U.S. Major League Soccer since 2002 and is currently a star for the team Olimpia of Paraguay.

Basketball and volleyball are also very popular sports up and down the country. Large crowds of spectators also gather for bullfights, which were introduced by the Spanish.

In the countryside, people come out to watch cycle races that are held in the mountains. The mountains are also ideal for white-water rafting, kayaking, and even volcano climbing!

▲ Boys play basketball in a Mayan-style court in San Mateo Ixtatan.

▼ Guatemalan children like these might be the first members of their families to get an education.

School Days

Many children in Guatemala never go to school, even though early education is free and is required between the ages of 7 and 14. Many Mayan children are too busy working with their families in the fields. Others live in remote communities too far from a school. Most teaching is in

MAYAN PEACE PROTESTOR

I n 1992, a virtually unknown Guatemalan woman, Rigoberta Menchú, became the youngest person ever to receive the Nobel peace prize. Rigoberta had written a book, *I, Rigoberta Menchú, an Indian Woman in Guatemala*, which told how she and her family had suffered during the long civil war. Her father, Vicente, had been killed by government forces while protesting about the war in Guatemala City. Rigoberta has called for the government official responsible for his death to be put on trial. She also fights for justice for the other victims of the war. Today, she is also a goodwill ambassador for the United Nations.

▲ Rigoberta Menchú holds a cross bearing her father's name in 2005, as she demands justice for his murder 25 years before.

Spanish, although some schools in the highlands teach in the local Mayan languages.

School attendance is better in the cities, but many students do not go past eighth grade because many high schools charge fees. Only a third of Guatemalan children make it through to the end of high school.

There are ten Guatemalan universities. They include the oldest college in the whole of Central America—the Universidad de San Carlos—which was founded in Antigua Guatemala in 1676.

Artistic Heritage

Guatemalans are very proud that they have two winners of the Nobel prize. One is Rigoberta Menchú, a writer and campaigner who won the peace prize when she was 33. The other is Guatemala's greatest

novelist, Miguel Ángel Asturias, who was awarded the Nobel prize for literature in 1967. His most famous novel is *Hombres de Maíz* (Men of Maize). More recently, Francisco Goldman won international praise for *The Long Night of White Chickens*, a novel set in Guatemala City in the late 19th century.

Music plays an important role in Guatemalan life. The local music is a mixture of Spanish, Mayan, and Garífuna styles. The most popular instrument is the marimba. A marimba is a little like a large xylophone and probably came from Africa. Fiestas and other celebrations always include marimba music, along with Mayan pipes. Marimba orchestras play at important events in Guatemala City.

▲ A big band of Mayan drummers and pipers plays at a fair in Quetzaltenango.

From the Fields

The food the Maya eat today is much the same as their ancestors ate centuries ago. A traditional breakfast consists of tortillas, eggs or beans, and coffee. A typical lunch might include a dish called "Caldo," which is made of chicken, broth, and fresh tortillas. For a special treat, Mayans might roast and crush cacao

leaves to make a rich chocolate coffee beverage. During the Mayan Empire, hot chocolate was a luxury drink. People believed it helped them stay healthy. It was very bitter, not sweet like it is today.

▲ Marimba players accompany masked Mayan dancers during an All Saints' Day celebration.

▼ Traders sell fruit and vegetables harvested fresh from the hills.

Rich and Poor

THE TWICE-WEEKLY MARKET in the highland town of Chichicastenango is a riot of color. Local Mayan women, dressed in vividly bright textiles, bring produce to sell at the market. Each village has a textile pattern, so the clothing worn by the women may identify where they live. Laid out on mats on the ground are all kinds of vegetables and fruit. People come to buy tomatoes, avocados, onions, chilies, apples, and flowers. There are also chunks of chalk for sale, which local people boil with maize to soften it.

The market is always busy. However, despite the money that changes hands, most of the people are very poor. Guatemala has one of the largest ranges of wealth of any country. Half the population earns just a tiny fraction of the income of the few richest families.

◀ **Mayan women wait in line to buy vegetables at the Chichicastenango market.**

POLITICAL CHANGES

▲ Official government ceremonies are carried out inside the National Palace of Culture in Guatemala City.

Today, Guatemala is a democratic republic. In 1986, the year the country officially returned to democracy after decades of military rule, a new constitution was introduced.

Although elections held since 1986 have been recognized as being fair, the Guatemalan military remains a very powerful force in the government. The country's power is concentrated in Guatemala City. The Maya have found it hard to get involved in the country's politics, and many villages have their own laws and rules. Each village has its own Council of Elders who run the village, hold trials, and pass laws for the local area. Since the end of the civil war, the Maya have won better representation. One of their victories is the right to be taught at school in their native languages.

Trading Partners

Guatemala's major trading partner is the United States. Its other principal trading partners are its neighbors. In 1991, Guatemala joined the Central American Common Market. This is an agreement with El Salvador, Nicaragua, and Honduras that makes trade easier. Guatemala also has deals with Mexico. Guatemala currently exports more than it imports. The main exports are clothing, fruits, coffee, and sugar. It imports fuels, machinery, transport equipment, grain, and fertilizers.

Country	Percentage Guatemala exports
United States	46.2%
CACM*	27.2%
Mexico	5.9%
All Others Combined	20.7%

Country	Percentage Guatemala imports
United States	34.5%
CACM*	9.7%
Mexico	7.9%
All Others Combined	47.9%

* CACM = Central American Common Market

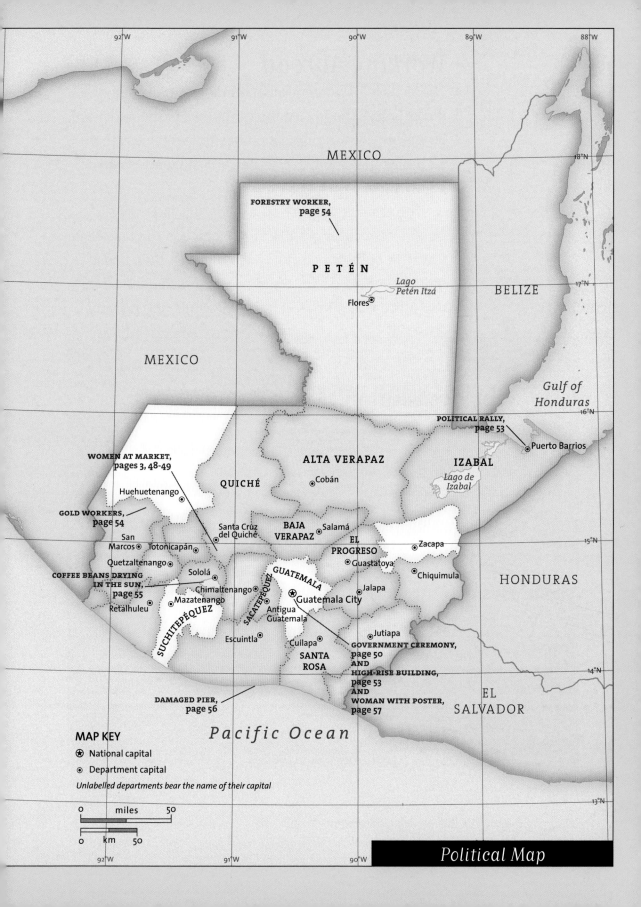

MEXICO

92°W
91°W
90°W
89°W
88°W

18°N

FORESTRY WORKER,
page 54

P E T É N

Lago
Petén Itzá

BELIZE

17°N

Flores ◎

MEXICO

Gulf of
Honduras

16°N

POLITICAL RALLY,
page 53

Puerto Barrios ◎

WOMEN AT MARKET,
pages 3, 48-49

ALTA VERAPAZ

IZABAL

QUICHÉ

Cobán ◎

Lago de
Izabal

Huehuetenango ◎

GOLD WORKERS,
page 54

Santa Cruz
del Quiché ◎

BAJA
VERAPAZ

Salamá ◎

EL
PROGRESO

Zacapa ◎

15°N

San
Marcos ◎ Totonicapán ◎

Quetzaltenango ◎

Guastatoya ◎

HONDURAS

COFFEE BEANS DRYING
IN THE SUN,
page 55

Sololá ◎

Chiquimula ◎

GUATEMALA

Chimaltenango ◎

Jalapa ◎

Mazatenango ◎

SACATEPÉQUEZ

Retalhuleu ◎

✪ Guatemala City

SUCHITEPÉQUEZ

Antigua
Guatemala

Jutiapa ◎

Escuintla ◎

Cuilapa ◎

GOVERNMENT CEREMONY,
page 50
AND
HIGH-RISE BUILDING,
page 53
AND
WOMAN WITH POSTER,
page 57

14°N

SANTA
ROSA

EL
SALVADOR

DAMAGED PIER,
page 56

Pacific Ocean

13°N

MAP KEY

✪ National capital

◎ Department capital

Unlabelled departments bear the name of their capital

0   miles   50

0   km   50

92°W
91°W
90°W

Political Map

Working Abroad

The richest 10 percent of Guatemalans have half of all the country's money. At the other end of the spectrum, 30 percent of the population has to live on less than $2 a day; the poorest 13.5 percent of Guatemalans barely survive on just $1 a day.

The difficulty of making a living has led many people to move from the rural highlands to Guatemala City. Life in the city is not much different than it is in most countries. There are shops and restaurants, high-rise office buildings and hotels. But it is getting very

HOW THE GOVERNMENT WORKS

The 1986 constitution created three branches of government. The country is run by the president with the help of the Council of Ministers. President Alvaro Colom Caballeros was sworn in on January 14, 2008, to serve a four-year term. Presidents can only serve for one term. Guatemala's vice president is Rafael Espada. New laws are passed by the Congress. Congress has just one chamber with 158 members. Members of Congress are elected every four years. It is part of their job to keep an eye on the work of the president and his or her ministers.

Guatemala's highest court, the Constitutional Court, has five judges who are elected to serve five-year terms. The Supreme Court has thirteen members who also serve five-year terms. These judges elect the president of the Supreme Court of Justice.

GOVERNMENT

EXECUTIVE	LEGISLATIVE	JUDICIARY
PRESIDENT	CONGRESS	CONSTITUTIONAL COURT
COUNCIL OF MINISTERS	158 MEMBERS	SUPREME COURT OF JUSTICE

crowded. It is estimated that around one in ten Guatemalans have moved abroad. There are more than a million living in U.S. cities, such as Los Angeles, Miami, and New York City. They have moved there to earn money, most of which they send back to their families in Guatemala. The money coming from abroad keeps the country's economy going. Economists think that around $3 billion is sent back to Guatemala each year. This is more money than the country makes from selling its top exports.

▲ President Caballeros holds a rally in 2007. Before the late 1980s, political rallies were illegal.

▼ A family dines at a new restaurant inside the first aquarium in Latin America, located in Guatemala City.

Finding Room for Crops

Although Guatemala grows a wide variety of crops, it actually has very little land that is suitable for farming. Only 13 percent of its area is used to grow crops. Most of the country is too rugged. The flat bottom of the Motagua Valley is a large farming area. The Motagua River provides water to irrigate crops. The warm Pacific lowland is also flat enough for farming, and its climate is perfect for growing valuable fruits and sugarcane. However, much of the rain forest in this region has

▲ Melted gold is poured into a mold at one of Guatemala's mines. Many Maya are unhappy about allowing mines on their land, which they believe is sacred.

been cleared to make way for fields.

Under the Ground

Most of Guatemala's fuel has to be bought from other countries, but there are a few small oilfields deep below the Petén. Small mining operations produce metals such as lead, zinc, and antimony. In the 1970s, the Lake Izabal region produced a lot of nickel, but the mines are now running low. In the last decade several gold mines have been set up in the western highlands.

Factory Work

During the civil war, few businesses were able to set

NATURAL GUM

One-third of Guatemala's land is covered with forest, and forestry is an important part of the economy. The country's most important forest products are hardwoods, balsam, and chicle. Guatemala is a world leader in the production of chicle, which is used to make chewing gum. Chicle is the sap produced by the sapote tree. It is a natural latex—a white liquid that becomes rubbery when boiled to drive off the water. Once it is clean, the chicle is mixed with sugar and flavorings to make gum.

▲ Deep channels are cut into a tree's bark to allow liquid chicle to trickle out.

up factories in Guatemala. However, since the late 1980s, the manufacturing industry has been growing. About 15 percent of Guatemalans work in factories.

Most factories are near Guatemala City. Many are small family businesses making textiles and packaging foods. Larger factories produce medicines, plastics, and chemicals. Many of the clothes sold around the world have also been made in Guatemala.

▲ Coffee beans harvested from mountain plantations are spread out beside Lake Atitlán to dry in the sunshine.

A Tale of Two Ports

Up until 1975, the main port in Guatemala, called Puerto Barrios, was controlled by the United Fruit Company. It was from here that bananas were once shipped to the United States. The Guatemalan

AGRICULTURE MAP

The highlands of Guatemala have fertile volcanic soil that is good for growing many different tropical vegetables and fruit. Agriculture accounts for 23 percent of the country's economy. Around half of the Guatemalan workforce of around four million people work in agriculture. The most fertile land is in the Motagua Valley and along the southern coast. Here, cotton, bananas, and sugar are grown alongside cattle ranches and rubber plantations. Farmers grow vegetables, corn, rice, beans, and wheat, in addition to raising pigs and poultry.

Coffee is grown at higher altitudes in the shade of larger trees, so the beans grow slowly and have more flavor.

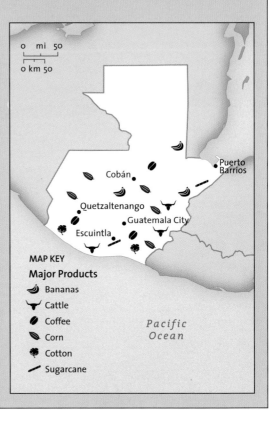

0 mi 50
0 km 50

Cobán
Puerto Barrios
Quetzaltenango
Guatemala City
Escuintla

MAP KEY
Major Products
- Bananas
- Cattle
- Coffee
- Corn
- Cotton
- Sugarcane

Pacific Ocean

▼ A fisherman cycles along a pier that has been lashed by a typhoon on the Pacific coast. Guatemala's ports are often hit by storms.

government decided to build its own port. It opened Santo Tomas de Castilla just 6 miles (10 km) down the coast. Despite being so close together, both ports are very busy. Puerto Barrios handles fruits and other crops, while its neighbor handles general cargo.

Finding its Place

Few tourists dared to visit Guatemala before the peace treaty was signed in 1996. Since then, tourist numbers have grown steadily. Most visitors come from the United States or El Salvador.

The Mayan weavings with their intricate patterns are one of the most popular purchases for tourists. Other Mayan crafts include bags made from the fiber of the agave plant and jewelry made from semiprecious stones and silver. Guatemala is the world's leading producer of jade, a beautiful stone that comes in a variety of colors. Wood carvings are painted with bright colors; wood masks, bamboo baskets, and mats are also made for sale to tourists.

In 2006, tourists spent more than $1 billion in the country. Most visited Tikal and took trips into the jungle. The Guatemalan government hopes that one day its country will rival its neighbors Costa Rica and Belize as popular destinations. Visitors will see that Guatemala has recovered from its violent past and is a country full of history with a great future.

A CRUSADING BISHOP

Guatemala's bloody history in the second half of the 20th century had many villains and heroes. One hero was Monsignor Juan José Gerardi Conedera, a bishop who criticized the military regime that ran Guatemala during the civil war.

In 1998, the bishop released a report that showed that most of the 200,000 deaths of the civil war were caused by government troops. Two days after the report appeared, Gerardi Conedera was murdered. His killing became a turning point in the ongoing struggle between the people and Guatemala's military. In 2001, three army officers were convicted of the archbishop's murder. It was the first time in Guatemala that serving army personnel had been put on trial.

▲ A human rights protester rolls up a poster of Gerardi Conedera after a rally to remember his death.

Add a Little Extra to Your Country Report!

If you are assigned to write a report about Guatemala, you'll want to include basic information about the country, of course. The Fast Facts chart on page 8 will give you a good start. The rest of the book will give you the details you need to create a full and up-to-date paper or PowerPoint presentation. But what can you do to make your report more fun than anyone else's? If you use your imagination and dig a bit deeper into some of the topics introduced in this book, you're sure to come up with information that will make your report unique!

>Flag

Perhaps you could explain the history of Guatemala's flag and the meanings of its colors and symbols. Go to **www.crwflags.com/fotw/ flags** for more information.

>National Anthem

How about downloading Guatemala's national anthem and playing it for your class? At **www.nationalanthems.info** you'll find what you need, including the music and words to the anthem in English and Spanish. Simply pick "G" and then "Guatemala" from the list on the left-hand side of the screen, and you're on your way.

>Time Difference

If you want to understand the time difference between Guatemala and where you are, this Web site can help: **www.worldtimeserver.com**. Just pick "Guatemala" from the list on the left. If you called someone in Guatemala right now, would you wake them up from their sleep?

>Currency

Another Web site will convert your money into quetzals, the currency used in Guatemala. You'll want to know how much money to bring if you're lucky enough to travel to Guatemala: **www.xe.com/ucc**.

>Weather

Why not check the current weather in Guatemala? It's easy—go to **www.weather.com** to find out if it's sunny or cloudy, warm or cold in Guatemala right now! Just type Guatemala City into the search box at the top of the page. You can then select one of several cities from around the country. Next to today's weather you'll see Sunrise/Sunset information, Wind, and Humidity. Scroll down the page for the 36-Hour Forecast and a satellite weather map. Compare your weather to the weather in the Guatemala. Is this a good season, weather-wise, for a person to travel to Guatemala?

>Miscellaneous

Still want more information? Simply go to National Geographic's World Atlas for Young Explorers at **http://www.nationalgeographic.com/ kids-world-atlas**. It will help you find maps, photos, music, games, and other features that you can use to jazz up your report.

Glossary

Altitude a measure of how high land is above sea level.

Civil war when two or more groups living in the same country fight each other for control of all or part of the territory.

Climate the average weather of a certain place at different times of year.

Colony a region that is ruled by a nation located somewhere else in the world. Settlers from that distant country take the land from the region's original inhabitants.

Communism a system of government in which a single political party rules a country with the job of ensuring that wealth is shared equally among all people.

Culture a collection of beliefs, traditions, and styles that belongs to people living in a certain part of the world.

Democracy a country that is ruled by a government chosen by all its people through elections.

Dictator a leader who has complete control over a country and who does not have to be elected or re-elected to office regularly.

Economy the system by which a country creates wealth through making and trading products.

Endangered at risk of dying out.

Exported transported and sold outside the country of origin.

Forest canopy the region in a forest located at the tops of the trees.

Geography the study of Earth's surface.

Habitat a part of the environment where certain plants and animals live.

Hardwood wood that is very dense and tough. Most hardwood trees grow very slowly compared to softwood trees.

Imported brought into the country from abroad.

Inlet a large bay or similar area of water that is surrounded by land on three sides.

Irrigate to bring water from a river or well to dry farmland so crops can grow.

Limestone stone made from the remains of seashells and other chalky substances.

Pilgrimage a journey made to visit a religious shrine.

Plantation a large farm or estate devoted to growing one crop.

Plateau a high, flat area.

Plumage the feathers of a bird.

Roman Catholic a Christian who follows the branch of the religion based in Rome, Italy.

Sinkholes deep holes in the ground created when caves collapse; sinkholes are often filled with water.

Species a type of organism; animals or plants in the same species look similar and can only breed successfully among themselves.

Union a political agreement between two or more countries—or states—so that they cooperate in trade, war, and other matters. Sometimes they act as a single country.

Bibliography

Dendinger, Roger. *Guatemala*. Philadelphia, PA: Chelsea House Publishers, 2004.

Markel, Rita J. *Guatemala in Pictures*. Minneapolis, MN: Lerner Publications, 2004.

Sheehan, Sean. *Guatemala*. New York, NY: Marshall Cavendish Benchmark, 2009.

Stalcup, Ann. *Guatemala in Colors*. Mankato, MN: Capstone Press, 2009.

http://news.bbc.co.uk/1/hi/world/americas/country_profiles/1215758.stm (General information)

http://www.authenticmaya.com/authentic_maya.htm (historical information)

Further Information

NATIONAL GEOGRAPHIC Articles

Saturno, William. "The Dawn of Maya Gods and Kings." NATIONAL GEOGRAPHIC (January 2006): 68-77

Web sites to explore

More fast facts about Guatemala, from the CIA (Central Intelligence Agency): https://www.cia.gov/library/publications/the-world-factbook/geos/gt.html

The resplendent quetzal is a much-loved symbol of Guatemala. However, they are difficult to see in the wild—even many Guatemalans have never seen one. This Web site contains videos of the colorful birds. Take a look: http://ibc.hbw.com/ibc/phtml/especie.phtml?idEspecie=3335

The ruined city of Tikal is full of Mayan buildings. Find out more by taking this virtual tour of Tikal at: http://www.destination360.com/tikal/guide.htm

Rigoberta Menchú is one of the most famous living Guatemalans. Find out more about her and why she won the Nobel Prize at: http://nobelprize.org/nobel_prizes/peace/laureates/1992/tum-bio.html

The United Fruit Company had a huge impact on the history of Guatemala and the rest of Central America. This Web site outlines its history: http://www.unitedfruit.org/chron.htm

Ricardo Arjona is Guatemala's most successful recording artist. He has worked as an architect and teacher and was a professional basketball player.

However, for the last 20 years Arjona has been making music. Take a listen at http://www.ricardoarjona.com

See, hear

There are many ways to get a taste of life in Guatemala, such as movies and music. You might be able to locate this:

The Guatemala Post
Read the news in Guatemala in this weekly English-language newspaper: http://www.guatemalapost.com

Guatemalan radio
Listen live to several Guatemalan radio stations at: http://www.surfmusic.de/country/guatemala.html

El Silencio de Neto (1994)
Guatemala's first commercial feature film tells the story of a boy called Neto during the military takeover of the government in 1954.

Index

Credits

Picture Credits

Front Cover—Spine: Heather Perry/NGIC; Top: Raul Touzon/NGIC; Low Far Left: Otis Imboden/NGIC; Low Left: David Evans/NGIC; Low Right: Roy Toft/NGIC; Low Far Right: Bobby Haas/NGIC.

Interior—Alamy: Danita Delimot: 59 up; Gianni Muratore: 3 left, 36-37; Associated Press: Rodrigo Abd: 53 lo; Corbis: Yann Arthus-Bertrand: 11 lo; Bettmann: 35, 45; Owen Franken: 55 up; Arvind Gary: 15; Bob Krist: 32 up; Daniel LeClair: 54 up; Danny Lehman: 21 up; Charles & Josette Lenars: 30 up; Sergio Pitamitz: 40 up; David Pocon: 53 up; Reuters: TP, 30 lo, 42 lo; Ulises Rodriuez: 56 lo; Galen Rowel: 2 left, 6–7; Studio Eye: 22 up; Jorge Uzon: 47 up; Getty Images: AFP: 44 lo, 57 lo; Hulton Archive: 33 lo; MLS: 43 lo; Travel Ink: 12 lo; NGIC: Tibor Bognar: 3 right, 48–49; Kenneth Garrett: 28 lo, 33 up, 44 up; W. E. Garrett: 12 up, 14 up; Jacob J. Gayer: 34 up; Patricio Robles Gil/Minden Pictures: 23 up; Martin Gray: 2–3, 24–25, 40 lo; Bobby Haas: 11 up, 14 lo; Giles Greville Healey: 13 lo; Luis Marden: 31 up, 34 lo, 38 up, 46 up, 54 lo; George F. Mobley: 26, 28 up; Terry W. Rutledge: 29 lo; Joel Sartore: 18 lo; Joel Scherschel: 5 up, 10 left, 43 up, 50 up; John Scofield: 41 right; Brian J. Skerry: 23 lo; Roy Toft: 21 lo; Steve Winter: 2 right, 16-17, 47 lo; Konrad Wothe/Minden Pictures: 20 lo.

For more information, please call 1-800-NGS-LINE (647-5463) or write to the following address:

NATIONAL GEOGRAPHIC SOCIETY
1145 17th Street N.W.
Washington, D.C. 20036-4688 U.S.A.

Visit us online at www.nationalgeographic.com/books

ISBN: 978-1-4263-0471-2

Printed in the United States of America
09/WOR/1

Series design by James Hiscott, Jr.
The body text is set in Avenir; Knockout.
The display text is set in Matrix Script.

Front Cover—Top: A Guatemalan girl standing in front of colorful Mayan textiles; Low Far Left: Carving of Mayan sun god; Low Left: Volcan de Agua as seen from Antigua Guatemala; Low Right: The Resplendent Quetzal; Low Far Right: Aerial view of Pacaya Volcano.

Page 1—Descendants of the Maya fly a traditional giant paper kite as part of an annual festival; Icon image on spine, Contents page, and throughout: Guatemalan fabric

Produced through the worldwide resources of the National Geographic Society

John M. Fahey, Jr., *President and Chief Executive Officer;* Gilbert M. Grosvenor, *Chairman of the Board;* Tim T. Kelly, *President, Global Media Group;* John Q. Griffin, *President, Publishing;* Nina D. Hoffman, *Executive Vice President, President of Book Publishing Group;* Melina Gerosa Bellows, *Executive Vice President, Children's Publishing*

National Geographic Staff for this Book

Nancy Laties Feresten, *Vice President, Editor-in-Chief of Children's Books*
Bea Jackson, *Director of Design and Illustration*
James Hiscott, Jr., *Art Director*
Grace Hill, *Associate Managing Editor*
Rebecca Baines, *Project Editor*
Lori Renda, *Illustrations Editor*
Stacy Gold, Nadia Hughes, *Illustrations Research Editors*
R. Gary Colbert, *Production Director*
Lewis R. Bassford, *Production Manager*
Nicole Elliott, *Manufacturing Manager*
Maps, *Mapping Specialists, Ltd.*

Brown Reference Group plc. Staff for this Book

Volume Editor: *Tom Jackson*
Designer: *Dave Allen*
Picture Manager: *Sophie Mortimer*
Maps: *Martin Darlison*
Artwork: *Darren Awuah*
Senior Managing Editor: *Tim Cooke*
Children's Publisher: *Anne O'Daly*
Editorial Director: *Lindsey Lowe*

About the Author

ANITA CROY earned her Ph.D. in Spanish and Latin American studies at University College, London, United Kingdom. She has traveled extensively in Latin America and has written a number of books for children and young adults on various Latin American countries.

About the Consultants

EDWIN J. CASTELLANOS is the director of the Center for Environmental Studies at Universidad del Valle de Guatemala where he also directs the Geographical Information Systems (GIS) laboratory. His research interests include mitigation projects and adaptation processes to climate change, management of natural resources by indigenous communities, and monitoring of forest cover using remote sensing. He is also a consultant with the United Nations Development Programme (UNDP) on issues of climate change and its effects on Guatemala.

MATTHEW TAYLOR is an assistant professor in the Department of Geography at the University of Denver. He has been conducting research in Guatemala for the last 15 years. His research interests include the impact of electrification on firewood consumption, how migration to the United States changes land use, the environmental impact of the civil war, human population and biodiversity, human modification of the highland environment, and water resource management. He also involves undergraduate students in community-based research in rural Guatemalan communities.

Time Line of Guatemalan History

B.C.

ca 9000 Hunter-gatherers begin living in the Guatemalan highlands.

ca 1000 People settle in villages and begin growing crops.

ca 800 Villages develop in the tropical lowlands of the Petén, including Nak'be, El Mirador, and Tikal.

ca 400 The town of Kaminaljuyú becomes an important trade center in the Maya highlands.

ca 200 Citizens of Tikal begin to build a large masonry platform that will eventually hold numerous pyramid temples. The platform is now called the North Acropolis.

A.D.

ca 250 The Maya reach the height of their power: it will last for some 750 years.

ca 260 The Ilopango volcano erupts, forcing people from the southwest highlands and disrupting trade networks. The region gradually loses status.

562 Calakmul overthrows Tikal to become the dominant power in the central area.

695 Tikal defeats Calakmul; two great temples are built on the North Acropolis.

ca 900 The Maya empire begins to shrink for reasons that are not fully understood; cities are abandoned and the Maya split into smaller groups.

1280 The Quiché establish a small state in the highlands.

1400

1410 The Quiché take control of most of the highlands and parts of the Pacific coast. They build magnificent stone temples and a ball court in the central Mexican style.

1480 The Quiché empire disintegrates and continues as a small kingdom.

1500

1523 Spanish explorer Pedro de Alvarado reaches the highlands.

1527 The Spanish found Santiago de los Caballeros de Guatemala in the southern mountains.

1530 Alvarado defeats the Quiché and their allies; the Spaniards take control of almost the entire southern Maya region over the next 10 years.

1541 Santiago is destroyed by a volcanic eruption. The Spaniards build a new capital nearby, now known as Antigua Guatemala. It becomes one of the most important cities in the Americas.

1542 Carlos V of Spain bans forced labor in the Spanish empire to limit the power of landowners.

1560 The Spanish create the Captaincy-General of Guatemala as part of the viceroyalty of New Spain.

1570 Highland Maya authors write the *Popol Vuh*, a collection of myths.

1600

1697 The Spanish conquer Itzá Maya, the last independent Maya city.